Twisted Vows

Marie Doreathy

Paperback: 978-1-965632-99-4
eBook: 978-1-966652-12-0
Library of Congress Control Number: 2025900231

This is a work of nonfiction.

Ordering Information:

Prime Seven Media
518 Landmann St.
Tomah City, WI 54660

Printed in the United States of America

A Tribute to Hollie Gazzard

Hollie had her life ahead, loved by her family and friends, her work colleagues and all who knew her. She was in a relationship with a young man who was jealous and controlling, Hollie was murdered by him in front of her work colleagues.

She was soon to be twenty one.
Her life she led was full of fun.
If she had known what was going to be,
For in our future we cannot see.

Her greatest ambition in her life,
To be a hairdresser for which she strived.
A beautiful young lady for all to see,
Loved by her friends and family.

For life can be cruel and so unfair,
Her life cut short what did he care,
God took you early, one of the best
Now dear Hollie you are at rest,

R.I.P

Permission given to me by Hollie's Father Mr. N. Gazzard. O.B.E , The Hollie Gazzard Trust.

Acknowledgements

To my close family and friends.
My daughter and my siblings.
Thank you for your encouragement and support
and making me believe that I can overcome
any doubts about writing this book.
Special thanks to my friend Lee who
helped and checked my grammar.

Preface

Having never written a true story before,

I felt compelled to share this with you.

This story is about my sisters marriage what she has had to endure in her marriage to the present day.

There are so many women and men who are trapped in a controlling coercive relationship, which leads to physical and emotional abuse. This behaviour gives the perpetrator power over their partner making it difficult for them to up and leave and end the relationship.

Too frightened to confide in anyone, they put up with the relationship rather than speak out.

"In the name of God, I take you to be my husband/ wife, to have and to hold from this day forward, for better, for worse, for richer, for poorer, in sickness and in health to love and to cherish, until death do us part."

Broken Dreams. Broken Promises

For better, for worse, for richer, for poorer, in sickness and in health, to love and to cherish, till death we do part.

This is my solemn vow.

I have written these notes as it tells of some harrowing experiences I have endured in my marriage.

Will these writings have any bearing on what my future will be? I don't know at this time in my life

It all began when I was just 14 years old. Was love blind?

I did not understand what would lay ahead for me.

I was brought up in the East End of London. My parents, siblings and I were raised on a council housing estate. My parents could not afford to buy a house, so like other families in the area, we were housed by the local housing authority.

My friends and I grew up in the 60's where we used to hang around the flats with lots of other young people our age. I remember clearly a lad just 4 years older than me, passing me on the stairwell and saying something to me. I answered him back and then the next thing I remember, he was hitting me around the face. I went back indoors and was crying my eyes out. This should have been an early warning sign as this lad turned out to be my future husband! What made me get together with him?

My older sister at this time would have been 17 years old and had her own friends who she went around with.

My education was good. I went to the local RC secondary modern school. I left school at the age of 16 with 9 CSE qualifications.

I took on a good job at a Stock Brokers in the City of London where I loved working. I had been working for them for a number of years.

Chatting to a friend one day, we decided that we would travel abroad on a working holiday.

At the age of 18, I was invited to a friend's party. I met one of the young men who used to live in the same block of flats as me. I didn't realize at first but he told me he was the young lad who had hit me across the face when I was 14. He seemed very nice and we started dating. He was kind to me and bought me flowers and small gifts. I told him what I planned to do and he was not very happy. He said the thought of losing me was unbearable to him.

My friend and I then headed off on our jaunt abroad. I was there for 3 months and during that time he wrote to me constantly telling me how much he missed me and couldn't wait to have me back home. I didn't know at the time that his Mum had written all the letters he sent me because he was dyslexic.

Into our third month of enjoying our summer holiday, my friend and I were offered a job working as nannies for a family in Rome. I had only been working as a nanny for 3 weeks when out of the blue, the young man I had been dating turned up. He persuaded me to return to England with him, convincing me that I didn't like the work I was doing. He had booked a return ticket back to London. He told me he had made arrangements for us to be married. I had no say whatsoever in the arrangements. We were married 9 months later.

The morning after our wedding, having been given lots of presents and money as gifts, I said we should sit down and sort out what we were going to do with the money. He told me to mind my own business and that it was nothing to do with me and he needed the money. Again, I had no say in this. All the wedding gifts we had received, he went through and said why did I need so many items. He told me he was giving them to his sister who was getting married a few weeks later. He reminded me that it was him who made all the decisions and I was to mind my own fucking business.

I was 2 months pregnant when we got married. During our first year of marriage, he hit me on several occasions. When I was 8 months pregnant, we had an argument and he pushed me down a flight of stairs. I could have lost the baby.

He walked out and during the next few days I decided to leave him. I contacted my sister and brother and asked for their help in moving me out and back in with my parents. Two days later, he came home and pleaded with me not to leave him and promised me that things would change for the better. He bought me a gold bracelet as a peace offering and told me how much he loved me. Again, how stupid I was. I should have realized then that this marriage was doomed from the start. "You have made your bed now lie in it" I was reminded by his mother. (old cow).

As the years passed, there was constant abuse, both mentally and physically.

I went on to have 3 more children but was still trapped in a marriage from hell. There was no way out.

2004. A very special year for various reasons as things unfolded.

British Legion disco to celebrate the New Year. Off I go with his Mum, my daughter and her friend. He was ill in bed, so he said. He is just a miserable man. Sad and pathetic and not a bit social. He only likes to mix with his own gambling friends.

Oh yes. He is ok to go on a holiday to the continent with his friend. He still calls me every day to check on what I am doing.

Peace and quiet with him not around. Why can't every day be like this? It is up to me to change my life. Turn it around for the better. Get rid of him.

Where shall I go? My siblings have their own lives and families. I don't want to worry them.

Off he goes. Where to? He doesn't say. Nothing to do with me. I should mind my own business so I am reminded by him. He has now been gone for about 5 hours. He returned home, nice as pie to me. That evening he made love to me. It was ok but sometimes I have no feelings for this man.

Next morning, he showed off ranting and raving, saying he had no money. I don't understand how one minute he can be a shit head and the next minute nice as pie.

He decided he now wants to go to a race meeting and stay overnight as the horse he has a share in is running at another venue. Of course, he said he had no money but still magically comes up with money to place his bets. His horse ran but came 5th so no winnings for him. What a waste of money having a share in an old nag that never comes anywhere and is sometimes last at the post.

Sitting there all peaceful I turned on the TV to watch Fawlty Towers, one of my favorite programmes. He decided that he now wants to watch football. No compromise. Selfish pig. Told me I was very rude and I was not to talk back to him but to keep my gob shut.

He was going off again. I normally have to pack his bags but this time he decided that he will pack them himself. Off he goes with the miseries as things don't go his way.

He decided that he is going to go to every race meeting. Every day to a new meeting in another town.

He said that he needs to get his money and this is very stressful for him. I said you never beat the bookies, you'll lose all your money. They are the only ones that come out winning. Again, he tells me to shut my gob or he will shut it for me. Well off he goes. He loves every minute of it

A New Year. Let's see what this year brings.

January. He argued with me last night. He has no sympathy for me. I suffer from a bad back and I have varicose veins in both legs. He told me that I was using this as an excuse to have a rest and told me to get to the kitchen and clean up the dishes. Only 3 dishes to wash! He told me I was a sad old cow and very much like my Mum. Also, I like to mark in the tv magazine the programmes I want to watch. Again, he told me how sad I am.

Weather very bad outside. I had to go to work to do my cleaning job. I asked him nicely if he would drive me to work. He refused as he said that he had to stay in as his friends would be phoning him and he had to wait in for their calls. I suspect it is a bit of wheeling and dealing. He doesn't tell me what he gets up to, and I should mind my own business as It's nothing to do with me. I had to walk to work in the freezing cold, hail and bitter wind. Living by the coast it is always a lot colder.

He is so cold and heartless towards me. I sometimes wonder if our marriage will last another year. We had sex that night but again I had no feelings towards him.

Weather bitterly cold outside. Luckily, I am not going out today. He decided he is going off again to the races. He tells me he has no money, yet he always seems to have enough to gamble on the horses.

He has taken to his bed. He has a bad cold. Serves him right. No wonder he is ill, going to the races despite having bad weather.

Again, he has stayed in bed. He is still unwell. Of course, I have to run here and there for him. Get him his tea. Bring it to his bed. Serve him his lunch. Serve him his dinner. Go down to the betting shop and place a bet, having to venture out in this cold weather.

It seems he has made a quick recovery. Today he is off again to the races. Had a big row this morning about how much money there is in the bank account. He did not like what I said to him. There should have been more money in the account. His temper got the better of him and he screwed up the bank receipts. He said that from now on he was going to put the bank account in his name and that I would not have any control or any say in what goes on with the finances. I told him to do what he likes and started to walk away from him. He was shouting and screaming at the top of his voice. Our accommodation is a rented flat above the local dental surgery. All the patients and dentists could hear him shouting his head off. He turned around and said "bollocks to the lot of them" in a very loud voice. He didn't give a damn about all the shouting. I am sure they heard every word and the bad language out of his mouth. He is just so foul mouthed and doesn't give a damn and couldn't care less what people think. I am positive he suffers from schizophrenia, taking after one of his uncles. Is it hereditary I wonder.

Since my last entry we have had several more rows. His cold has turned into a bad chest infection and he blames me for this. He has spent the last two weeks in bed watching racing and placing bets over the phone. It is our daughter's birthday and I decided to go into Brighton with her and five of her friends to get away from the moaning bastard.

He has soon recovered from his bad chest infection and he has been to the races all day and he came home coughing. He still has his bad cold. What a shameful selfish pig. I sometimes say to myself I hope he drops dead and my life would be better without him. I would be free at last to live my life in peace but unfortunately that's not how things pan out in life. As his mother once told me "you've made your bed now lie in it"

My youngest son came down for my daughter's birthday. We decided to have a Chinese meal that evening and again he was his miserable self and hardly spoke to his own family.

It was bitterly cold in the flat. I was in the bedroom getting ready to go out. I had the heater on and he came into the bedroom and asked why I had put it on. He was shouting and said that he paid the bills and I should sit in the cold. He started shouting his head off and got hold of the heater and threw it across the room. I said I feel the cold more because of my medical condition. I have an underactive thyroid which the cold can affect. He was swearing his head off at me. He told me that I was making it up and I didn't have this medical condition and I was talking a load of bollocks. He told me I should have kept my mouth shut and from now on he will shut it for me.

We decided to visit a family friend. We had been invited to her birthday party, She lived about two hours away and we decided to take his Mum with us. She is elderly and doesn't get out much. At least now I wouldn't have to sit in silence. I can chat away with her. He started again and told me he wasn't going to speak to me at the party. He spent all evening talking to everyone else and not a word to me. When we got home, he went straight to bed. Eventually, when I went to bed, he was snoring his head off. Why doesn't he just fuck off I say to myself.

Today we had a family funeral. As we were leaving, he asked me what I had in my handbag. I replied, my gloves, my book to read in the car and I had a blanket to put over my knees as it was freezing outside. He called me stupid and said I didn't need the blanket as it was warm in the car. He said I was like my Mum, acting like an old lady bringing a blanket with me. He also brought up the fact that when I was out shopping and I see an elderly person sitting on a bench, I go up to them and have a conversation. I enjoy chatting and I am sure they are happy for a bit of company and a good old chat. I'm sure it makes their day. My Mum died at the age of sixty not eighty. What a horrible man he is.

I said to him, "well what do you want to do? Tie me to the kitchen sink." He said if I was chained, I still wouldn't do any housework and would leave everything dirty. I told him to change the record. He then turned round while he was driving, grabbed my wrists and the car swerved and he hit me in the mouth. He said he didn't give a shit about my teeth. Previously I had an accident when I fell down an unmarked hole in the street where the local authority who had been working there had failed to put up a barrier or a warning sign. I fell flat on my face and lost some of my teeth. I was in a pretty bad state. After being treated at the A & E and seeing a dentist, I had to have two root extractions and I was now wearing a plate with four new temporary teeth. My mouth was still sore and I was in agony for the rest of the day. I was shoving painkillers down all day long but what did he care if I was in agony or not. He is a sadistic bully.

Our daughter was at school and I asked him if he would go and pick her up as I was not feeling very well, especially after the tooth accident. My mouth was bleeding badly. He told me I was selfish and that he had to stay in as he was waiting for a telephone call from his friend and that I should go and meet her from school. It was freezing cold outside and I had to put a scarf around my mouth to keep out the cold. He is heartless. What did he care, the bastard? I wish I could be stronger.

Next morning, he didn't speak to me at all. He headed off to London. He arrived back late that evening and demanded a sandwich and tea. He shoved these down his gob (pity it didn't choke him) then went off to bed.

Next day I went to see a family friend who is ill in hospital. He said that while I'm out, I have to post some mail for him. He's too lazy to walk to the post box. Oh yes, your fucking slave will do it for you. What a fool I am.

What a carry on. Just passing each other in the house without saying a word. How stupid am I putting up with his childish tantrums. I asked him if he would like some breakfast and he said "Okay". The day continued without a word and he went to bed early that night. I stayed up late until I knew he was asleep. I didn't want any physical contact with him.

I cannot have any say or express my opinion. He shouts me down and calls me stupid and selfish. He says I should have learnt by now, after thirty years of marriage, I was to keep my mouth shut and not to have an opinion on anything. I cannot get my point across. What a battle I am faced with. Why should I be treated so badly by him? All the time I don't speak to him I am getting no grief, it is easier for me to keep quiet.

Another week of silence. The only time I spoke to him was to ask what he wanted to eat. Maybe I should poison his dinner and make him sick as a parrot. I should have told him to get his own dinner.

One evening he came home late. I suspected he had been seeing someone else, a friend of a friend. She can have him and put up with all his crap. Talking of crap, I was putting the washing on and I noticed that his underpants were stained.

He must be seeing her or has he been satisfying himself having a J.Arthur Rank.

Still not talking and he tells me I should put an advert in the local paper, and let everyone know I am not speaking to him. He is worse than a spoiled child. He said he was not going anywhere and that it suited him to do what he wanted. He said he did not have to apologize to me for what he had done and he would never apologize.

Our son was getting married later in the year and I told him he should not spoil his plans. He tells me to go and shows me where the door is. He says I shouldn't get too cocky with him and to take the smile off my face otherwise he will take it off for me. I told him if he hurts me again, he would go to prison and our daughter would be on her own. His answer was that I had better do as I was told then. Our daughter was standing at the door listening. I wonder where we go from here. I am willing to put on a brave face for the sake of our son's wedding. I will file for divorce next year. Let's see what happens in the next few months.

I am not getting any snide remarks and it is pleasant in the house at the moment. He has been out every day, going to the races and spending all he can on the horses.

Nice and peaceful at the moment. He is not picking on me and not moaning about anything and not coming near me in bed. He must be getting his oats elsewhere. Maybe he is making love to one of his horses! Let him carry on.

What is he up to? Not that I care actually. He has gone away for the weekend. He said he had to go away on business for someone who is retired. What business is he up to? I dare not ask as he tells me to mind my own business. Well, let him get on with it.

A family friend passed away in hospital after a long illness. He has kept himself busy taking control, sorting out his friend's flat and possessions, and making the funeral arrangements. He told me not to interfere. I expect he didn't want me to in case he found any money lying around in his friend's property. The funeral went well and his friend had a good send off. Lots of family and friends came.

He has now told me he wants to talk to me as we haven't really spoken for a while. I told him I was fed up with the way he treats me and abuses me. I am not his punch bag and why should he keep getting nasty with me. I have put my point forward and he has told me that he will never change and I have to put up with the way he is. Like it or lump it. Surely this will make me sit up and think about our marriage. After this talk, he pulls me towards him and starts to kiss me passionately and now he wants to make love to me. I let him have his own way. I am not arguing about this.

Peace and quiet doesn't last long with him. He's now back to his normal self, arguing, shouting and moaning about what I have and haven't done. "Well why don't you do something to help me for a change" I ask. He tells me my place is in the home and not to be speaking to my friends or family as I should put him first. Yet again he tells me I am selfish. He has lost a lot of money on his gambling and, as usual, he takes his frustrations and his anger out on me.

Tomorrow he is off on holiday with his friend and he tells me he doesn't want to go near me before he goes away and doesn't want to share a bed with me. I have to do all his packing for him. I have to make sure all his shirts and other items of clothing are neatly pressed and packed. I should let him do his own packing. Sometimes I could kick myself for being so stupid. I expect it is the fact that I have always done it and in my mind I can't change. Hooray. He has now gone and I can relax and meet up with my girlfriends for lunch and go to my bingo. In fact, I can do what I want without being quizzed every time.

He is back from his holiday. He tells me he is now going away for a few days to Newmarket for the racing. He is now back from the races and has lost a lot of money.

I believe he has another woman as he always leaves me to unpack his weekend bag when he has been away, but this time he puts two pairs of his underpants into the laundry basket. Before I put these in the washing machine, I check the pants and they are full of stains. Again, they are not skid marks but sperm stains. I am positive he has another woman.

In bed that night, he wants to make love to me but halfway through he loses his sex drive and starts a heated argument. He tells me he is going off me and that I am too mouthy and I should be the same as I was when we first got married. Well, what about him? It works both ways. What do you want to do? Bash me up all over again as you did from the very first day we got married. I could kick myself. Wake up I say in my mind. He tells me I am always taking but never giving. He is a selfish bastard.

Winter has now passed so hopefully with Spring in the air, I can get out more after being stuck indoors.

I had a lovely weekend away with my sister, my young daughter and my daughter's friend.

He went off to the races at Newmarket on Friday and came back on Saturday evening. He told me he had won a lot of money. Off to bed we went and he kissed me and decided he wanted to make love to me but he couldn't get a stiffy. I wondered if he had been seeing his girlfriend this week and had enough with her.

This week he is skint.

It won't be long now until our son's wedding. He had £5000 and paid it into our son's account as a wedding present. I asked him where the money had come from and he told me it was none of my business and not to ask questions. Obviously, I don't mean anything to him. He treats me like a skivvy and expects me to be there at his beck and call.

Tonight, in bed he wanted to make love to me again. I have no feelings towards him and I faked my orgasm as I just wanted it to be over as soon as possible.

This week he asked me why I hadn't been near him. I explained I had my period.

He has no money this week but he has decided to go off to Spain for 4 days. Well, where did the money come from, I asked myself. He told me not to call him while he is away. He came back and had only just walked in the door when he started on me again, saying that I should think about our marriage and that he wanted to go off on his own and find somewhere else to live. Hooray. Maybe he will go. I won't be so lucky as he will not find another slave to do his running around, cooking, washing, cleaning and taking the abuse that he lashes out at me.

He asked me this morning to go to the shops and get the daily newspaper. I refused and he got the right arse over this as I wouldn't jump when he asked me to. He is old fashioned in his ways and says a woman's place is in the home. He doesn't believe in the modern woman. He said that his mother did as she was told and I should do the same. He said he was not going to change for anyone. He said all my friends are a bad influence on me and that I have too much to say for myself. I ask God to help me make the right decision and wonder what the future holds for me.

With my son's wedding coming up, I cannot think straight and how can I deprive my children of their father, not that he has been much help anyway. I asked him for a trial separation but he would not agree to that. He said that once he goes then that's it and he would never speak to me again. It makes me wonder again if he has another woman.

There would be a lot of sorting out to do. He said the decision would be mine and mine alone whether he leaves or stays. It's just so that he won't look like he is the bad person in front of his family and friends.

Something odd is going on with him. He is always going up to London to see his friends and is going to the races constantly.

I have to decide what I would be missing if we do end our marriage. Can I cope on my own financially? Do I need him there to support me in any emotional decisions? What will our sons and daughter think of me leaving their father?

How will my friends react if I should decide to separate?

Could I live without the sexual intimacy we have although I hate him at times?

Would I be better off on my own?

Decisions, decisions. What shall I do?

Will he give up his home comforts?

Who will do his washing, ironing and cook his meals?

Will he go and live with his Mum? I don't think so.

I feel quite alone. I am not with him most of the time anyway. Conversations are few and far between as he's always watching the tv and the horse racing. Decisions are made by him but he always wants me to do the work involved. Our son is getting married soon so all decisions are on hold at the moment.

He is off to Spain again. I wish I could afford to pay someone to follow him to find out what he is getting up to out there. At least I would then have proof. Maybe he has another bit of fluff out there! When he is away, I like to go to bingo and meet up with my friends.

Now he is back from Spain and again he starts the questioning. He tells me that he doesn't like me going to lunch with my friends or going to bingo. He tells me that my place is in the home, cleaning and getting rid of clutter and reorganizing the kitchen.

He tells me that I have too much in the cupboards and should get rid of unwanted items. He just wants me to stay at home every day and not have any independence whatsoever.

My brother has come over on holiday for a week and is staying with my sister and I have arranged to meet up with him. I told my brother about my teeth and he has kindly given me some money towards a new set. I am not to tell my husband about the money as he would take it from me.

Tonight, Friday, is bingo night and I told him I was going. He got the right hump about me going out. He has decided now to ignore me. Next morning, he still has the hump with me and says he is now going off to Newmarket races. I told him to have a nice time and his reply was "Don't worry I will" and tells me it is my fault he is going as I went to bingo last night. He came back from the races that evening and said he wanted to discuss things with me. He proceeds to tell me that I have had no respect for him since the day we got married and that I tell everybody our business. He says when he tells me to do things I should jump and do them without any arguments and when I refuse, I am being disrespectful towards him.

I need to get my new teeth sorted out after my bad accident and I tell him that I will get them done privately. He tells me to get them done on the NHS. Well, I know the reason for this. I had been given compensation by the local authority. He took most of the money and left me with just enough to get them fixed on the NHS which was half the price of having them done privately. Well, this is the reason why. He wants money for his gambling. Bastard. I am too weak to argue over this. He calls me selfish once again.

He has some loose change on the side and I decided to go and get the daily papers and I took the change. He then asked me why had I touched his money I had no right to and that I should have asked his permission to take it. He tells me I am rude and not to touch anything of his. I argued that it was unimportant and why was he going on so much about it. I threw the change back at him and went off to the shop with my own money to get the papers. When I came back, he had gone out. That evening he starts again. I have gone off to bed and he tells me I should have shaken the pillows as I don't shake them enough. What on earth has got into this man. I don't know if I can handle this for another twenty years or however long our marriage lasts.

We have been invited to a wedding and at the evening reception he is chatting to a lady I do not know. He greeted her in a friendly manner and he was talking to her for ages. I wonder if this is his bit on the side. I wonder if there is something going on between them. He never introduced me to her and I asked him why. He tells me that she was drunk at the time and that she was a friend of one of his cronies. She drinks in one of the public houses where his friends hang out and every week, when he goes to London, he always drinks in this pub. I'm sure he meets up with her there. I'll have to keep a lookout for any signs that something is going on. I checked his underpants and there were some stains on them. Not skid marks but other stains.

Next day we did not speak much. He now tells me he is going to Portsmouth to meet somebody but wouldn't tell me who. I wonder if it is someone arriving by ferry from Spain. Maybe he met a woman out there and decided to meet her on the ferry. He arrived home late that evening. When he went to bed, I checked his underpants again and found further stains. I will have to keep my eyes open and listen for anything unusual he may be talking about on the telephone.

Today he brought his friend round for the day and demanded that I stay in and cook lunch and dinner for them both. He then tells me they are off to Spain for two weeks. Good I say to myself. At least now I will have two weeks of peace and quiet.

Today he is back from his holiday in Spain. The first thing he said when he came home was that he wanted to tell me something. In his controlling manner, he proceeds to say that from now on I could do what I liked and if I encounter any problems, I am not to go to him for help but to go to my friends and immediate family to sort them out. He did not want to be involved in my life and asked if I wanted him to pay me for any sex. He is doing his best to control me in any way possible. I ignored him but he kept on and on. In the end he got fed up as I would not comment and just walked out. That evening he came back but not a word was said. He went off to bed and he is now loving towards me and we had sex.

Next morning, I was busy ironing and he asked me to make him a cup of tea. I asked him to wait a few minutes. Well, he couldn't wait and got up and went to the kitchen and made his own tea. He didn't even ask me if I wanted a cup. Selfish pig.

He is now back in and has thrown all my magazines in the bin and told me the kitchen was like a tip. He then tells me I am banned from ironing in the front room as it disturbs him watching the television. Next morning, we had a big row and I said he was trying to control me. He then screamed at me, saying he would show me what controlling was and that I should pack up all my part time jobs, ironing, cleaning etc. and he would tell me what and when to do things. He said that I was selfish and ungrateful for all he does for me. He said I wanted to be a modern woman in the 21st century but he didn't want me to be like that. He wanted me to be there for him to get his meals. He treats me like a skivvy.

It is Sunday evening and he is not feeling well. My young daughter tells me he has phoned for an ambulance as he has bad chest pains, a racing heartbeat and cold sweats. The ambulance people carted him off to hospital. Serves him right for being an utter schizophrenic. He is just a complete arsehole. I hoped they would keep him in for a week or two but they just kept him in overnight, What a turn up I wasn't expecting this at all. Yes, pay back to you, you bastard.

The hospital told him he had a high risk of heart trouble as his father had died of a heart attack. They treated him for high blood pressure and sent him home with some pills. Pity they weren't horse pills. He thinks more of the horses than his wife!

Within a week, he is back to his old self again. My sister was having a big family party and he forbade me to go. He asked me why I wanted to see my family anyway, and his word was final.

My Marriage from Hell

Many years of marriage
Many years of hell
Too frightened to leave
Too frightened to tell
The bruises don't show
The pain is still there
No one to talk to
No one to care
My body is broken
My mind is too weak
He tells me I am selfish
He is just a control freak
A life of misery
From when I was young
I sit back and ask
What on earth have I done
No one to talk to
No one to tell
My life continues
To be a living hell

The arguing continues. I told him he should take some Viagra and he said it wasn't his problem, but the problem was with me. He says I shouldn't go to bed wearing an old woman's nightie but should wear something sexy and revealing. He tells me I should only wear one ring on my finger. He is jealous, as his friend, who is now deceased, gave me a beautiful ring to wear. He did not think it was right to wear it and I should act my age. Well, fuck me. What has a ring got to do with acting my age? The jealous pig. Not only that, but he says I should not wear my gold chains around my neck, as they make me look too young.

He says that in an emergency or a crisis, my family would not help me in any way. I am sick and tired of him picking on me all the time for no apparent reason. He just wants to order me about at every level he can.

Today we had an appointment with a consultant about our young daughter who has ears that stick out. My husband tells me to keep my mouth shut and not to ask the doctor any questions. He wants her to have the operation before our sons up and coming wedding. The doctor tells us that this is not possible as our daughter would be in bandages for a few weeks, and it was out of the question. I asked the doctor lots of questions and when we got outside, he had a go at me for speaking up and said I should have kept my gob shut. What a Jekyll and Hyde. That night he wants to have sex. How can I have feelings for him when he talks to me like I am a bit of shit.

He now accuses me of having an affair with a friend and said I was acting strange. A girl friend of mine was ringing me up a lot and arranging for me to go out. He then tells me I cannot go to my sister's party as he doesn't like her. He says when I see her, I come back all cocky and answer him back when I should be keeping my mouth shut.

I took out a loan with the bank so I could get a nice outfit for my son's wedding. He asked me for half of it and I refused. He wanted it to pay off a gambling debt. He hasn't spoken to me all week! Today he is still angry as I refused to give him the money. He tells me to do what I want and as soon as the wedding is over, I can fuck off otherwise he would. He tells me I have no principles and I should be loyal to him and not listen to my family.

He has had a lot of bad luck recently with the gambling and he is up to his limit on the credit cards. He owes thousands of pounds. He will never be free of his horse racing gambling and he will never learn. We had a beautiful house and he sold that. We had a small amount of equity in this, and he took the lot and gambled it away. He told me it was nothing to do with me.

I was going to offer him my beautiful diamond bracelet if he was that short of money, but I have decided against it as it's the only security I have. He will never be free of his debts.

The wedding went off well and everyone looked stunning in their outfits. The wedding reception went to plan. It was at a local college, and it was a beautiful place to have a wedding.

Now I am feeling lonely and not feeling well. I have the flu and couldn't do my cleaning job as I was too ill. I have to get motivated as it will soon be Christmas and I have lots of presents to buy and shopping to do. He refuses to take me shopping. He drives and I don't. I should have learnt years ago. I did try but I had a minor accident while learning and he told me to give it up and he would run me anywhere I wanted to go. Well, that didn't last long! He now refuses to take me shopping etc. I have to lug it back home in all weathers. My back aches so bad from carrying the heavy bags.

Christmas has been and gone and it has been very difficult these last few weeks. He has had a lot of bad luck with his gambling and is now in a lot of trouble with people. He is very moody, especially with me. He is now going on about the dishwasher, asking why it is not emptied as soon as it is finished, and am sick of arguing with him.

He now tells me that he will have to borrow money from our young daughter's savings to get him out of trouble. Rather than take her money, I tell him to sell the diamond bracelet instead, as he needs the money urgently.

He has spent the last few days lazing about in his dressing gown and not getting dressed. He has the right arse as he has no money to go to the races. He has now said he will give up the gambling and maybe get a job. I can't see this happening in the near future as he has been gambling since he was a teenager. I told him how old and miserable he is and he says he has no intention of changing for me or anyone else. If he had saved all the money he had spent on horse racing, he would have been a millionaire by now. He has nothing to show for it. He sold our lovely home and we now live in rented accommodation, spending a lot of money each month on rent and robbing Peter to pay Paul.

He then tells me I have no respect for myself. I had been watching a programme on tv called The Office and he said it was dirty and disgusting. He said he would not have watched a programme like that in front of his mother. He then said I should be at home, cooking his meals and not going out to bingo.

I had been having a good sort out in my kitchen cupboards and had sorted out some nice things for my sister who worked for a local charity. He asked me what the items were for and when I told him he took every single item and smashed them to bits. If they had been for someone else, he would have left them, but as they were for my sister (he hates her) he said she was getting nothing. I told him they were for charity and his reply was "fuck the charity and fuck your sister".

I have an ironing job which I do each week for a friend. She delivers the ironing to me. He now says I can no longer do her ironing and to pack it up completely. It is a little bit of extra money if I need to buy anything for myself. Well, now! have decided to go to her house and do her ironing there instead. That's one thing he can't stop me doing. He just doesn't want me to have any extra money for myself, but to just rely on the money he gives me each week for the shopping.

He has now taken the diamond bracelet that he gave me for my birthday, and sold it so that he can have money for his gambling habit.

Today I told him I was thinking of taking up line-dancing. He replied that I should be in the kitchen, cleaning and cooking and be there for when he needs a cup of tea or his meals, and that I should not be going out with my friends. He now accuses one of my friends of being a lesbian as she often calls me. My friend looks after her husband who suffers from Dementia and Alzheimer's. She calls me often for a bit of support. She looks after her husband twenty-four hours a day seven days a week and now and again she needs a bit of time on her own.

I am sure my husband is the devil's child. His mind is so wicked and he just doesn't have sympathy for anyone, not even his own mother who is aging. He has lost the plot.

He tells me to shut up or he will pour a cup of tea over me and I will end up in hospital. I will have to be careful what I say as I don't want to upset him.

Our middle son is gay. He came down to see me while my husband was abroad on holiday. When my husband calls me, he wants to know what our son is doing while he is away. He says "I expect you have been telling him all that's been going on". Our son is so kind. When he decided to tell us he was gay, my husband went mad, although I know he is mad anyway! He told me that I was not to tell anyone on my side of the family that our son is gay. My son called his auntie (my sister) and he told her. She told him she would support him in any way and not to listen to other people who had a negative attitude. It was his life and not to take any notice of these people. My son is loved dearly by my sister.

My husband was not willing to listen to our son. He has always been the defiant one of our children. When he was younger and going to university, his father wanted to take all his university money from him for his gambling, but our son refused. His father then started screaming and shouting at him and told him he was a selfish little brat and he was typically like his mother's side of the family.

Our son doesn't have any time for his father. He has made a good life for himself. He had a good university education. He left university with a top degree and got himself a top work placement in a very good company. He has a lovely partner who is in the legal profession and they are very happy. They now have two young children. My husband says that it is morally wrong for two men to bring up children. What an old-fashioned attitude he has. If he had been married to a suffragette, she wouldn't have taken all the crap that I have to endure. He has brainwashed me and made me think I am inadequate and not capable of anything. I realize now that he keeps me short of money so that I rely on him. What a bastard. Maybe in my next life I will meet a nice man and be happy and live my life to the fullest without worrying where the next penny is coming from. What a fool I've been. If only we could see into the future.

Life As It Is

Life seems so unfair at times
If only I could see
What lies ahead for me.
In life that's not meant to be
Things are sent to try me
In good times and in bad
Events that happen in my life
Most times drive me mad.
I should live my life and be thankful
For the things that I have got
When my life is over
These things won't mean a lot
I should be happy for the sunshine
The wind, the rain and the snow
Be happy just to see a new day
For tomorrow I'll never know
I am happy with my family
And my good friends that I've got
I am happy for everything
Even though I don't have a lot

He is now back from his holiday and limping badly. He tells me that he has gout in his left foot. (Pity it doesn't fall off!) He has gone off to bed early as he is unwell. A few days later, he is back to normal. Going off to the races every day, gambling and spending every penny he has.

Why am I staying with him? I don't love him anymore. He is so cold and calculating in his behavior towards me. I have lost something inside me, and I know it will not come back. I believe this is down to his bullying, controlling me, shouting, swearing and mental and physical abuse. I then ask myself why do I stay? It is easy for people to say just get up and leave him, but where would I go? Are my friends going to let me stay with them? I know that certain members of my family would let me stay, but do I want the upheaval of all that. I know that I could stay with my sister. She has been through a lot of traumas herself recently. Her partner of 25 years committed suicide, and this has affected her greatly, but mentally she is strong and will come through this. I wish I could be strong like her. I know deep down that he would find me, and my life would be even more miserable. He would hound me day in and day out.

He is in deep money trouble again. He owes a lot of interest on a loan he took out and he now has to pay it back. He has 3 years to pay it back and his payments are high each month. Oh, what a stupid man, and I have to put up with all the crap that goes with it as he has no money. He tells me to stop nagging and blames me.

He now accuses me of having an affair with the local workman. The workman's wife wrote a note to my husband and told him that it was me that her husband was having an affair with. He told me that he has spies all over the town. This is the second time now he has accused me of having an affair with another man. He has lost it big time. Is he so insecure or is he hiding his own guilt, I wonder?

Today he has gone on holiday again and he is calling me everyday to check up on me. What for I do not know. He tells me he has his spies out on me. He is a total crackpot.

The local workman was always kind and polite to both of us. At times when he came round to do work for our landlord, he would see how my husband spoke to me and treated me in front of everyone. He didn't care who heard him shouting and screaming and he said he didn't give a fuck. I always found the workman easy to talk to and if we bumped into each other while I was out shopping, he would always stop, and we would have a good old chat. He was a nice man but not my type. Mind you, anyone who was nice to me was a thousand times kinder and considerate to me than my husband.

I had my mobile phone, and my husband took it off me every day to check who had called and who I had called. The phone was in his name, and he paid for it. He said he had a right to check what I was up to. One day while I was out shopping, I bumped into our workman friend. He gave me a mobile phone and told me that if I was ever in trouble or needed help, to call him straight away using this phone. He said he was concerned for my safety, and he did not trust my husband who may get violent towards me. I did not tell him my husband had beaten me up in the past. I had to keep this phone in my handbag so that my husband wouldn't find it. Unfortunately, early one Sunday morning, after a big row with my husband, he went through my wardrobe and my handbags, and found the phone. He then started accusing me again of having an affair with the workman. He went crazy and hit me in the mouth, got me on the bed, put his hands around my neck and said he was going to kill me and the workman. He hurt me badly and said he was going to get a gun from a friend and come back and shoot me. Before he left, he rang my sister at 7.30am. She was with her new partner, and he told her that he is going to kill me and asked her what she knew about my man friend. Of course, my sister was not aware of anything going on. If there had been, I would have told her. I know she would have said "good luck to you".

While he was out of the house, I rang my sister, and she told me to get out of the house as quickly as I could and to get a train up to my son's house in London and she would come and pick me up from there. My sister contacted my sons, and they were concerned for my safety. While my husband was out, I left and got the train to my sons. My sister came and collected me and took me to her house.

All that afternoon, he was ringing me and pleading with me to go back and discuss the situation with him. I agreed to meet him at his sister's house which was not far from my sister.

It was late in the evening. My sister, her daughter and her daughter's husband dropped me off at his sister's house and said they would wait for me until I was ready to leave. My husband told me he would change, and things would be better, and he was sorry for hitting me.

I told him I needed time to think about our marriage and I would give it a lot of consideration. I got up to leave and got as far as the front door when he told me I was going home with him. I refused and said that I was going back to my sisters. He started punching me and got me up against the wall and tried to choke me. My sister, her daughter and her husband jumped from the car and came to my rescue. He punched her daughter and started fighting with her husband. My sister called the police and two officers turned up. He was abusive to them and also to my sister's daughter. He said to her that he hoped both her and her mother would die hand in hand from cancer. He accused her daughter and her husband of trying to get rid of my sister and said they wanted her dead so they could get all her money. The whole neighborhood was out listening, and he told them all to fuck off and it was none of their business. What a wicked bastard he is. The police officers gave him a caution and told him to go home otherwise they would arrest him. He then left and shouted back to me that he would get me no matter what. I left with my sister and we went back to her house.

During the following week, he was constantly ringing my sister on her landline. She refused to answer it. I discussed the whole situation with my family and decided that I would see a solicitor about starting divorce proceedings against him. We made an appointment to see a solicitor in the vicinity where I lived. My husband had spoken to me a few days previously and said that he wanted to see me to talk things over. He said he would change, and he would treat me more kindly and do more things for me. He had asked our sons to come down and be present so that he could discuss any issues that he and I had. I told our sons lots of home truths and about the way that their dad had abused me both mentally and physically in the past and more recently. He brought up the subject of my friendship with the workman.

He has been making cups of tea for me in the morning and bringing them to me while I was still in bed. Well, that's the first ever. He has been loving to me all week, telling me how much he loves me. I cannot at the moment tell him I love him. Has he really changed, or will things get back to normal? Making things right with my family will, unfortunately, take a bit longer. He now wants my sister to come down so that he can tell her how he feels about the whole situation, but I know my sister will never speak to him again. She said that he is a wicked person, and after the wicked things he said to her daughter, she will never ever forgive him, even if he was the last person on earth.

Three weeks on and, oh yes, he is now getting back to his normal self. Controlling me, shouting, screaming and using bad language towards me. At what price have I got him back? He calls all the shots and is quick to criticize me. He is like a parrot on my shoulder, asking me what time I am going to bed and telling me not to watch the television as it is ruling my life. He is there all the time. Taking me to my cleaning job, coming to pick me up and watching my every move. He tells me he will never trust me again and says that he was the wronged person, and it was me who caused all these problems.

I tell him that my good friend has arranged a girl's night out and that I was invited to this. He hit the roof and told me that I am being selfish again. He says that as he is doing most of the work in the house, why should I be going out enjoying myself. He brings up the subject of our workman friend and asks me why I don't pick up the phone and call him. He is just a jealous nutter. He doesn't like me having any friends at all, whether they are girls or men. I must devote all my time to him. I have done a terrible injustice to my sister who has been so kind to me.

My husband checked my phone and some message had come from our workman friend. He now wants to know how the workman got the phone number. So that he wouldn't hit me, I told him that my sister had been speaking to the workman and she had given him the number. I lied to save myself. He now blames my sister for all that has gone on in our marriage. He says that she has interfered all these years and that she is the scum of the earth and how dare she ruin his marriage. He has told our sons and his brother and his wife, never to speak to my sister again.

I went to see a friend of ours who has a disabled daughter. He looks after her twenty-four hours a day, seven days a week. My husband went potty and was shouting his head off. He said I was not to be friends with any man, whoever he was. I was not to speak to him again otherwise he would go and kill him.

He wanted to make a fresh start. I agreed to this for my own peace of mind. I told him that I was very immature when we married at such a young age and that a lot of resentment had built up inside me. I said I was not able to cope with the way he had treated me all these years and I needed to find love again. He has changed a lot this week and has been a great help to me.

He has been hoovering, cleaning and even washing up the dishes.

He now tells me I have no principles at all, and I am selfish. He then tells me that my friend is abusing his daughter as she is disabled and cannot speak up for herself. What a wicked and corrupt mind and attitude he has. He should go to hell when he leaves this world and I hope that God will judge him and send him down to the devil.

We had a big row and he then took everything out of the bottom of the wardrobe and threw it down the stairs. I decided to sleep in the spare bedroom, and he shouts and screams at me to come down and clear up the mess he has created. He is so insecure or is it that he is slowly losing his control over me.

He now tells me that I have to choose between him and my family and I should never speak to my sister again. If I choose her then the marriage is over for good. I felt so guilty about what I had done to my sister and I couldn't cut her out of my life. I told him I couldn't choose. He accused me of all sorts of things and how dare I go against him. He told me that I have to make up my mind by the evening otherwise he would tell everyone in the family about the way I treat him. He forgets how he has treated me for the last thirty years of marriage. I've put up with him controlling me, abusing me mentally and physically and not having any money. Having to watch every penny I work hard for as well as looking after my sons and my daughter.

He has now decided he needs a holiday, so he is off abroad again for ten days or so. It was lovely being on my own. No shouting, screaming etc. Peace for a week or two.

Oh yes. He is back and he has now decided that we should go out jogging early every morning. I find this very tiring, and he tells me I am too slow and not trying hard enough. We are both eating healthier and are cutting down on bread and all fatty foods. I find it very difficult to lose a bit more weight. I will continue to eat more sensibly.

He had stopped his gambling for several weeks and has now decided to have just one more bet. Money is still short, but he seems to have found the money to go on holiday. I know he is of unsound mind, and he finds it very hard to talk about things unless it is to do with the horses.

He has told me that I'm not allowed to use the house phone to call my sister and if I want to call her, I must go to the local telephone box. He tells me that he doesn't want me to see any of my family ever again. I can only see them if he gives me his permission. He doesn't want my older brother coming down to see me when he comes over on holiday. My brother stays with my sister, and they normally come down to visit for a day. He tells me to tell my sister that they are not allowed in this town. Who does he think he is?

I have had to withdraw some money from one of my credit cards as he needs the money to pay a bill. He said he would pay me back as soon as possible when he gets some cash in the New Year. He now tells me that he is thinking of going bankrupt. He says it is all my fault he has to do this.

He has taken the mobile phone from me and said that if I want my daughter's old phone, I can have that to use. I refuse and tell him that if I want to call my sister, I will go to the public phone box. He gets annoyed and I tell him that as I no longer have a mobile and there is an emergency, then they can contact him. He is fuming at my response and now wants me to have the mobile back so that he can contact me whenever he wants to check on me. He has realized that if I haven't got a mobile, he can't keep a check of where I am or where I am going.

That evening he came home very late. He woke me up and started accusing me again of having an affair. It was 2am in the morning. He pulled the covers off me and moved close to my face. He said he was very close to hurting me because he was brewing up all his emotions inside because I refused to cease all contact with my sister and my family. I had a terrible night's sleep and was so tired the next morning. I must stay strong for my own peace of mind.

He has now decided that he is going away on holiday again. Once again, he tells me that I have to use the public phone box if I want to speak to my family. He says he will be checking my mobile when he returns, to see if I have obeyed him.

He is now back from his holiday, and as soon as he walks in the door, he starts again with his accusations. He just doesn't want to move on. The last few days have been mental torture with his anger and aggression. He has now started shouting at me about getting his dinner. He has been ill in bed, and I didn't take his dinner up to him. He has to have his dinner on time every evening at 6pm. He screams and shouts at me saying that instead of having his dinner at 6pm, I had taken it to him at 8pm. He said I had ignored him all day and couldn't care less about him. He liked his dinner on time, and I had only been thinking about myself. He told me not to bother. He came down from the bedroom and went to the fridge and took everything out and threw it in the bin. He asked me why I kept leftover food, and that it was all rubbish. I had kept a piece of beef for myself that was left over from the day before. He threw this on the floor and jumped on it. He said he couldn't care less what food he threw away. He then went and made himself a sandwich. He ignored me for the rest of the evening. I stayed out of his way, but he then tried arguing with me again. I cooked dinner that evening, and he said that he didn't like what I'd cooked him. I felt like saying "well cook your own dinner, you ignorant pig" but if I dared speak to him like that, God knows what would happen. The only way I am going to have a quiet life is if I ignore his tantrums and keep my mouth shut.

It's the 6th day after Christmas, and I decided to take the decorations and lights down, but he decided he wanted it done his way. Again, an argument started. He pulled down all the decorations, the lights and the cards off the wall and threw them in the bin. He then smashed up one of the chairs, breaking the legs off and the seat. I said to him "why don't you smash up the whole place?"

It took me ages to clear the mess up. He tells me to sleep in the other room as he doesn't want me sleeping in the same bed as him. I had a terrible night's sleep.

Next morning, before I go to my cleaning job, he wants to take me to the workman's house and to admit that I had an affair with him. I refused to go and needed to get to my work. Why should I admit to something I haven't done? When I came back that day, I had ironing to do as a second job. This I do indoors. I am shattered most days from doing these jobs and having to clean up his mess, while he lays in bed most of the day, lazy pig.

I went to bingo with my friend that evening and when I got home, he was in bed but not asleep. So again, he starts ranting and raving, telling me he is going to keep me awake all night until I admit to having an affair. I tell him I'm not admitting to something I haven't done. He then takes all the photos with my sister off the wall and rips them up. He then goes through my photo albums and again rips up all the photos with my sister in. He accuses my sister of being a cancer in his side, and that the only way she will be out of his life, is if he gets a knife and goes to her house and stabs her to death. He now decides he is leaving and packs his bags. He then tells me to fuck off out of the house. He hates my sister and says

I am selfish as I wouldn't do what he tells me to. Why doesn't he just go as he said he would. No, he needs me to be skivvy. Someone to punch, scream and shout at, and to be there to see him smash up anything he gets his hands on. Oh, why am I staying? I just don't know.

Am I so deluded that I think things will improve. I just don't know.

Next morning, he starts again, and wants me to admit that I have been unfaithful to him. I then decided to turn the tables on him and accused him of having an affair with a local woman. I said I had been told by one of his best friends that he had been seeing her, and that's why he came home on several occasions with stains on his underpants. Again, he goes mad and smashes up the bathroom and all my creams and bathroom accessories. It looked terrible. What a mess! He then took all my money and bank cards from my purse and said that if he was controlling this was how he would be. He said that he would stop me doing all my jobs and everywhere I went he would come with me to see what I was getting up to. He then threw my money back at me and told me to stick it. I said to him that if ever I won the lottery or came into some money, I wouldn't need him, and I would fuck off and live the rest of my life happy and without any aggravation from him. He left the house at midday. I cleaned up the bathroom and cleared away all the broken bits. He came back at 2pm and said that he wanted us to start over again and asked me to go with him to the D.I.Y. shop to replace all the items he had smashed up. He said he was laying down a few stipulations and that I was to obey him. These were that I was not to call my sister on the phone from the house. Not to talk to my friend who has a disabled daughter, and not to look or even glance at the workman. I must empty the dishwasher every morning and I must keep the place neat and tidy. He tells me it will be like we have just met, and we must try to respect each other's point of view and not to bring up the past for any reason. I decided to give it a go and to work at our marriage. The weekend was very pleasant, and he made love to me over the weekend. I think he was pleased with me. He is very clever, so I will still be on my guard, as I know he will be watching my every move. A good week for all of us. He went to the races a few times, and he gave me some money to spend on myself.

He lost all his money and now wants some money from the bank account!

My son and daughter-in-law came down to visit us, and he talked to them about buying a house. He said he would ask our three sons to help out. He decided to ask our gay son if he would consider getting a mortgage in his name. Our son refused, and he then asked our other son and daughter-in-law if they could give us a deposit to put down on a house if we could get one at a reasonable price. He has made an appointment with a debt collecting agency to see what they can do to help clear his debts. He is getting fed up with not having any money. Of course, he has given it all to the bookies. As I had said to him previously, no one beats the bookies. Gambling is a mugs game. I know he will never give it up, although he says he will. Never, never, never. He has been gambling since he was a teenager. I just have to play along with him.

He is not happy with our gay son because he refused to get a mortgage. He says to me that he will never get anywhere in life if he doesn't do things illegally now and again. How wrong was he saying that about his own son. He was angry because he could not manipulate any of our sons. He had lost control and power over them all. This is why he hates my sister. She would stand up to him. She once said to him "you married the wrong sister. You would have been out of my life by now as I would not put up with all the crap my sister has put up with". Of course, he didn't like that and told her that he remembered her from when she was young and that she was stuck up and never spoke to him. Why can't I be strong like my sister? Nobody will walk over her.

He is back to his old tricks again. I went to town to get some shopping and while I was out, I telephoned my sister from the public phone box. Prior to this, I ordered a takeaway meal from the local restaurant. He decided to call the restaurant to find out where I was. I collected the meal, and on my way home he was walking towards me ranting and raving and asking me why it had taken me so long. He accuses me again of speaking to the workman. I told him I had been talking to my sister on the phone and his reply to this was "bollocks, you are lying again". He says how dare I go to the phone box when he and our daughter are waiting for their meal. Again, he tells me I am selfish and put my sister before him. He says that he doesn't trust me as he had seen the workman drive past in the direction I was coming from and asked if I was speaking to him. He said that if he ever heard a whisper or I waved at the workman, he would do me in. He would smash me to a pulp and when he went before the magistrate, he would plead insanity, as he was under the doctor for depression.

He continued the argument all evening, and said that as I was now speaking to my sister, all his problems came back to him. I said "why are you bringing up the past again". He said he would only rest and be happy when my sister was out of our lives completely. I told him my sister would always be around for me. Next day, he started the row again. I didn't take much notice of his ranting and raving and saying how selfish I was. He said I was slipping back into my old ways. He said we should be together all the time, twenty-four hours a day, seven days a week. I asked him what about when he goes to the races as I have no intention of going with him.

He had been out and when he came back, he told me he had bumped into the workman's wife and they had a chat. She told him that her marriage was not going well. He then asked me if I felt sorry for her as I had almost broken their marriage up. I asked why I should feel sorry for her. I didn't feel anything. He then went berserk again and started shouting his head off. The next few days were dreadful. He kept on and on bringing things up from the past. I said that we should move forward otherwise we would not get anywhere. He has been miserable all week as he had no money to have a bet. He needed something to keep his mind occupied and the gambling had to be put on hold. He is not a happy bunny.

Today he is happy, as his friend has left him some money in his will. He has decided to use some of it to pay off some of his credit card debt. With the rest, he said he would take me on holiday. Well, that will be a first. He usually goes off on his own, or so he says!

We have been to the citizens advice bureau and they have worked out a plan with us to clear all his credit card debts. It involves offering all the credit card companies a small payment each month which we hope they will agree to. I'm not sure if this will work. He may have to be declared bankrupt as he owes a considerable amount of money. Over twenty-three thousand pounds! He just will not give up the gambling and this week he has lost over two thousand pounds on the horses!

He is still not happy with me. Every now and again, he tries to get me to admit I've been having an affair.

Today, I was going to my cleaning job and noticed the workman sitting in his vehicle. I stopped to have a chat with him. He was asking me how I was. The next thing, my husband appears from nowhere. I had been unaware that he was following me. He was shouting and screaming at me saying that he had now caught me out. He was screaming at me to go away. The workman was still sitting in his vehicle with the window open. My husband was trying his hardest to hit him and punched him in the face. He started smashing up his vehicle, pulling off the windscreen wipers and smashing the windows and windscreen. There was glass everywhere. The neighbors were out telling him to stop. They called the police and they came and took him away. He had badly injured the workman. He had broken his nose and he had cuts to his face and bruising to his eyes etc.

I had to go to the police station to make a statement, telling them the sequence of events and why my husband had beaten up the workman. I saw the workman at the police station and told him how sorry I was for my husband's actions. He told me that his only worry was that when my husband came back from the police station, he would start on me and I must take care. My husband was charged with criminal damage and actual bodily harm. The police told him he was not allowed home and he had to stay with a family member until the court case came up. He stayed with his brother for about a week and then came back home. I told him he wasn't allowed home and he stubbornly said who would know.

He has no respect for the law and doesn't give a damn about anyone. He was very angry with me and blamed me for what he had done. He tells me that I shouldn't have spoken to the workman and that I had gone against my word, making me feel very guilty.

My friend called me and I spoke to her for about ten minutes. He went berserk and said he was waiting for his tea. He wanted to know what I was talking to my friend about and why it had taken ten minutes. I said I had arranged to meet her for lunch, to which he replied "oh yes, to tell her all our business". He is obsessed. I cannot even have a conversation with my friend. He ripped the phone from its socket, threw it across the room and it smashed into bits. He said he would get rid of all the phones and I wouldn't be able to speak to anyone. He continued the argument into the early hours of the morning and stopped me from getting any sleep. Next morning, he started again, telling me I should not read a book or fall asleep in front of him. He says I only use him when I want him to do something for me. He says I must not call my friend, not even from the public call box and I was to put him first in our relationship. Again, he blames me for everything and if he gets a prison sentence, he says he will never forgive me as it is all my fault.

If I should walk away from the marriage, He said he would tell our sons and daughter never to speak to me again, and I would have no one for support. He thinks he can control everyone close to him, but he picked on the wrong one with my sister. She wouldn't stand for any of his nonsense. I tell him that I have my sister and my brothers. They tell me that whatever happens, they will always be there for me.

He has now gone away for the weekend, and I have arranged to go to my sisters to meet up with my brother and his wife and some close family friends. I had a lovely few days with my family. He calls me at my sisters and says he will collect me on his way back from the airport.

Next day, he quizzed me about my days away, asking me what I did and accusing me of having a nice time without him. He was shouting and screaming that I am not loyal to him and that I should not have enjoyed myself. He said he has had all the weekend to think about our marriage and he tells me I must have nothing more to do with my sister or our marriage is finished. He knows that whatever happens, my sister and my family will always be in my life and will always be there for me. He has not stopped nagging me all week. He demanded that I get my sister out of my life and that she is a cancer that has to be cut out somehow. He says he hates her with a vengeance for ruining his life these last few months and has never felt such hatred towards anybody in his life as he feels towards her.

My sister has an apartment abroad, and my eldest son and his wife have booked to stay there. My husband has gone crazy, swearing and shouting and saying that his son was not loyal to his father. He gets the cups from the kitchen, and smashes them all to bits. There is broken crockery everywhere and I have to clear it all up.

I am now sorting out my paperwork and neatly filing them away when he starts his ranting and raving again. He takes all the files and throws them over the floor. He said it was a load of bollocks me filing them away as he said at one stage, he would destroy the lot. I told him I didn't love him as he keeps smashing the place to bits and that he should go to anger management. I think it is a shrink he needs!

His family don't give two hoots about me and they don't want to get involved. I know I wouldn't get any moral support from them in the event of something dreadful happening. He told me I am his possession and belong to him and nobody else.

He has his court hearing today. He said before he went that he would get away with actual bodily harm and criminal damage and that more than likely, he would get a fine. How wrong he was. He telephoned me from the court and told me he's going to prison for a few months. Peace at last, but what will happen when he comes home. I will have to be on my guard.

If anything happens to me in my life or if I was in any danger from him going mad due to the things that have happened over the last few years, these notes may be used in a court as evidence against him. Should anything happen to my sister, these notes will tell that he wanted to harm her. He blamed her for everything, especially for advising me not to stand for any of his nonsense. She was telling me for my own good. He said I should be listening to what he tells me and not listening to my sister. He is a jealous and wicked man.

He has now gone to prison and I worry for my safety when he comes out. He will, of course, continue to blame me, but I have to stand my ground on two principles. I will never give up seeing my sister or any other member of my family. I will not give up my part time jobs as we need the money.

I will try to move on with him. If the abuse continues, I will have no option but to end our marriage. Should I leave him now or should I face the music? Only I can make that decision.

I need to be on my guard now and watch him very carefully as he will be released from prison soon. He still blames me for him going to prison. I must try not to upset him in any way, and not give him any reason to lose his temper. I am expecting the worst from him. He has now arrived home, and he wanted to hear all the news, if any. He checked all his mail. I cooked him his favorite meal and he went off to bed early after a long day traveling. It was late when I went to bed and he was asleep. He woke up and started to kiss and cuddle me. I fell asleep in his arms.

Now back home, he decided he would not eat a lot as he wanted to keep the weight off that he had lost in prison. Next day we had a meal in a nice restaurant as we were celebrating our wedding anniversary. The peace and quiet didn't last long. In bed that night, he started shouting and moaning about my family. He said they were no good and that I knew what I was getting into when I married him, and I was not to make excuses that I was naïve and immature and too young to make decisions.

Next morning, he started again, asking me if I had seen the local workman and saying that if he ever found out I had spoken to him at any time, he would be a dead man and he didn't care if he ended up in prison again. He said this was a warning to me. I told him I had not seen him and I was getting on with my life. His reply was "I think that man has learnt his lesson." His next comment was about my best friend. She is not married and has a daughter. He said how dare she give me advice on my marriage when she doesn't know what it's like to be married. He said she should mind her own business and concentrate on bringing up her illegitimate daughter. He then said he didn't want to hear my sister's name mentioned under any circumstances, and I was not to mention her in any conversations I had with his family or friends even if they asked about her. I have tried to keep calm and avoid any confrontations with him.

We decided to book a few days away and take our daughter and her friend with us. On the way he had a row with me as I needed to stop to use the toilet. We didn't speak for the next two hours of our journey. We arrived at our destination and the next few days were peaceful with no sarcastic remarks from him. We arrived back home four days later and he started to try and control me again. He was moaning about the dishes in the kitchen telling me that my place was in the kitchen washing up straight after dinner instead of leaving them on the side. My friend telephoned me, and I spoke to her for a while. As soon as I got off the telephone, he started again about the dishes and said I should not put my friends first. I have decided not to get into any confrontations with him and to keep my mouth shut. I don't want to upset him.

Someone has reported him to the local security office and he has pointed the finger at my sister. He was screaming and shouting and saying I should not discuss our personal life with her. I know there are many people who do not like him so why blame my sister. It could be anyone who has a grudge. He has turned a lot of friends into enemies and even his only brother doesn't speak to him. I know that as much as my sister loathes my husband, she wouldn't jeopardize my life.

It is my birthday and we are off to the local Chinese restaurant. He has no money so I decided to pay for the meal out of my birthday money. His cousin had been invited and he told me not to let her know that I paid as it would make him look small knowing that he had no money. That evening he starts again, telling me I am selfish and disgraceful and asking why I am putting him in an awkward position in front of his relatives.

He is gambling a lot online and losing a lot of money. He will never give up the gambling. He has no money and he has now decided he will go bankrupt as he owes so much money to various building societies and catalogue companies. When I mention anything to him, he tells me that I know nothing and I should keep my opinions to myself. He knows best and I should keep my mouth shut. He has now sent all correspondence, bank statements etc. to the bankruptcy assessor. He seems to think that he won't have to pay a penny back.

He continues to question me about where I go when I'm out shopping or I meet my girlfriends for lunch.

He has been collecting points on one of the store cards. I decided to use the points towards my weekly shopping. He said how dare I take his card without his permission, and that he was saving the points up for Christmas. He said I was penny pinching and I was just like my scabby sister and brothers and I was up to no good. He said he would never forgive or forget why he was sent to prison and he would take his resentment to the grave.

He has received a small amount of money from an insurance claim he made when he had a car accident and suffered severe whiplash. I asked him if he could give me an amount towards my credit card bill. He refused, saying I was only asking him to get my own back because he had a bit of money and I wanted to get my hands on it.

We had a massive row when he was shouting and screaming at me. He said he had been trying to telephone me and wanted to know who I was talking to. I told him I was talking to my sister as she was not allowed to call the house phone. He said he was going to have the landline disconnected so I can't speak to anyone.

The last few weeks have been tough, and I ask myself why. I have devoted my marriage to him and all I seem to get back is abuse. I have brought my children up the best I can, without any input from him. It is difficult for me to keep him happy as it is his nature to blow up at any time. He wants to show me he is the boss around the house. I try to stay calm.

Today he asked me what time I was going to my cleaning job and what time I would be back. I told him a time but decided to read the newspaper before I went. I went out later and consequently got back an hour or so later than I'd said and he hit the roof. He was shouting and screaming at me and I asked him what all the fuss was about, and told him politely to fuck off! He threw the shoe rack across the hallway and proceeded to kick it. He was shouting at me because I'd sworn at him. I told him I hear worse from him towards me. He uses swear words that I wouldn't repeat to anyone, for instance the four-letter c word I hate to hear anyone use. He left the house and was gone for less than five minutes when he rang me. He said how dare I speak to him like that and it was the last time I would do it or there would be more trouble than I bargained for.

His cousin has a holiday home abroad and he decided that we would go there for a week or two. As I don't like flying, he decided to drive instead.

He had a small amount of money left over from his insurance claim and he decided to have a bet on the horses. He lost all the money! He is now stressed out and said the horses have let him down. He blames everyone else for the fact he has no money.

His mother is very frail and can no longer look after herself. He has decided that he will move her in with us. He didn't discuss this with me and has said that it is no business of mine and he knows best. It's another way to control me. He tells me that she won't last long but I wouldn't be too sure of that. No one knows when their time will be up. God will take you when he is ready. She has now moved in and loves to sit by the window looking out and getting some fresh air. He has accused me of belittling him in front of his family because I spoke against him on the subject of his mother. He just doesn't understand how old people live and it is a big responsibility looking after her. Now all of this will fall on me. He was very angry and brought up the subject of me looking after my dad for only six months which was about twenty years ago. It was his idea and he only did it for financial gain. He went potty and said how dare I think like that about him. He went on and on about my sister reporting him to the DHSS and said why did I still speak to my scraggy sister after all she had done to us. He has no proof of who reported him. He has made so many enemies even within his own family so it could have been anyone. He was talking to me close up and I could smell his breath. I put my hands to my mouth and he went mad. He got a pot of hair gel and pushed it into my face very hard and then started rubbing it into my hair. I told him again to fuck off and I scratched his hand. He hit me on my head by my left eye. He was very angry and told me not to sleep in bed with him and not to have anything more to do with him.

Another day of trying to control me. He tells me I am talking too much to my sister, my sister-in-law and her children. He says I mustn't tell them about anything that goes on and shouldn't be passing messages between them all. I should discuss everything with him before telling them anything. He said that my sister and the workman are in contact with each other and that he gives her messages to pass on to me. He is talking through his arse as I have not set eyes on the workman.

A calm day today and things have settled down. He told me that he loved me and I said I loved him too. Maybe I do love him because he is all I have known my whole life. I have not been strong enough to stand up to him and I have let him rule and control me from the day we got married. What a fool I have been and how stupid I am.

His mother has been with us for a few weeks now and she has the onset of Alzheimers and short-term memory loss. She is moaning all the time and saying that she needs to see the doctor every day because of shortness of breath. She is vicious towards me and doesn't understand that we have to look after her as the other family members work all day. She eats and drinks little. She has been checked by the medical staff and they say she is very healthy.

The arguments have started again and he says I am not to meet any of my friends for lunch and I need to be at home to look after his mother. I am stuck here with her. I tell him that I need a bit of time to myself and need a break to meet my friends. Oh yes, he said. It's all me, me, me and you are a selfish cow.

He said that I want to be a 21st century woman and he doesn't like that. He wants me to be the little yes sir wife I used to be years ago. He threatened to smash my face in and he head butted me on the back of my head because I answered him back.

I made lunch for him and his mother. Before this, I had loaded the washing machine and it had now finished. He came to the kitchen and started shouting and saying why did I take the washing out of the machine before we had lunch. He said why did I leave the cupboard doors open and why did I leave the kitchen untidy. I told him I didn't want the lunch to get cold. He told me to stop my cocky attitude or he would take the smirk of my face and smash my face in. He then raised his fist to me and said I never do as he asks. He said I should have left the washing until later. I told him he needs help to calm his anger. That evening in bed, he said he was fed up with my attitude towards him. He said I would not do as I was told and things would have to change or our marriage was over. I was not brave enough to say ok let's finish it but then he would have put his mother in a home. I know that he and his family would not want that. I think the reason he wanted her with us was because he was receiving money from the state for looking after her. Oh yes. A bit more money for gambling.

He is the one who is a selfish bastard. He is full of insecurities about me and who I see and speak too. He wants to know everything about my family and yet he tells me not to speak to them. He is worse than a child. He stamps his feet and throws and breaks things in the house. Of course, with a child you can chastise them, and threaten to take the things they love away from them. With him you cannot give your opinion or stand your ground.

Christmas is almost upon us and he has no money. I have received my compensation from the fall I had previously and he wants me to pay off one of his gambling debts. I refused and told him that he shouldn't be gambling. Why should I pay off his debt? It's his, not mine. He says I am like my family, money mad and very selfish. If I had a pound every time he used the word selfish, I would be a very rich woman now. For over two days he was very angry with me. He said that marriage is all about sharing and I didn't want to share what little money I had with him. In temper he cut up all my credit cards to hurt me. He smashed my radio and threw cups into the sink. He went through papers in the kitchen and tore them up. I got angry and scratched his hand. H to me and hit me across the face and neck, leaving a red mark. One of my earrings came off, and I fell backwards on the kitchen floor and hurt my hand. I told him he was a fucking bastard and that our marriage was over. He said it was my fault and that I had made him do it. I shouldn't be so selfish. I left the house and went into town to use the public telephone box to call our son. I told him what his father had done. The next thing I knew was that he had followed me and he came up to the telephone box thinking that I was calling my sister. He started shouting again and told me to fuck off to my friend the workman. I went home and he continued shouting and screaming. He told me that he didn't mean to hurt me but it was my own fault. He said he was sick and tired of it and that he had no money. I am not sure about his state of mind as he loses his temper so quickly especially with his mother. I don't think he is the full ticket and he needs professional help. He won't admit he has a problem and blames everyone else.

Why has it taken me so long to do my ironing job, which incidentally, took me three hours or so. He accused me of being on the telephone and doing nothing. He was shouting his head off and wanted to know where I had been when I wasn't ironing. I tried to explain to him that looking after his mother, getting her dinner and tea, making beds etc. took time. He called me a liar, saying that I should have emptied the dishwasher. He said the flat was a tip and everywhere was filthy. He started putting things in the dishwasher, slamming the door and breaking some of my crockery. He then got all my letters, shopping list and camera, threw them across the floor then put them in the dustbin. He went off to bed in a bad mood!

Next day he is at it again, moaning and whining. I telephoned my brother early in the evening and while I was speaking to him, the impatient bastard started shouting at me to hurry up off the phone as he wanted his dinner. After 1 finished speaking to my brother, I told him that as we had our lunch late dinner would also be later. I cannot change things as I have to do so much for his mother. I said if there was any way he could make things simpler for me to let me know. I told him I would write down everything I do from when I get up, giving him a detailed description and time. He tells me to shut my fucking mouth up and not to back chat him or he will shut it for me.

The last couple of weeks he has settled down and for a change, there is no shouting or whining over things. He has taken me shopping to get some underwear for his mother. She needs more of this as she is now incontinent.

My grandchild has now arrived and it's a lovely little girl. I can't wait to see her. I will enjoy spoiling her and buying things for her with any spare cash I have.

I have spent most of today with his mother and she is driving me mad. She is so frail but I think she will carry on living for a few more years. She is very aggressive towards me and lashes out. I know it is the Alzheimers that makes her nasty but sometimes I cannot help myself, and I lose my temper with her. He tells me not to be so nasty to her and that I should just walk away when she starts. I wish I could walk away from both of them for good! His sister is coming from abroad so that will at least give me a break and ease my burden.

He is now sodding off on his holiday with his friend. Hooray, I say. No shouting or taking abuse from him for at least ten days.

Two lovely weeks of peace but it hasn't lasted as he is now back home, and as soon as he walks through the door, it all starts again.

Off he goes to the races. He has spent all his money and he has the right hump. He feels so sorry for himself. He decided to go to bed earlier than normal in the late afternoon. I carried on with some jobs around the house. I went to the bedroom to put some clothes away and he said I had woken him up. He told me to fuck off and leave him alone. Later that evening I was speaking to my friend on the telephone when he started shouting at me, telling me I should have been clearing up the house after he had his dinner. I was taking out the rubbish bag and he grabbed it and it split, spreading the rubbish all over the floor. He said it served me right and he had now made more work for me. He got a glass of water and threw it in my face. I called him a bastard and he said I was too lippy and had too much to say for myself.

Next morning, I was in the kitchen having my breakfast and he started again. He was screaming and shouting at me, saying I was too selfish and only thought about myself. He said I didn't give him any respect. He told me to fuck off and go and see the workman who has a terrible mouth because I liked talking to people who swore. Look who's calling the kettle black. He should listen to himself. He threw all the coats on the floor and stamped on them, saying that I didn't care about his things. He said I was not to speak to him again unless it was to have a sensible conversation. I told him he is the one who has no respect for me by throwing a glass of water in my face. He said he could do what he likes as I don't do what he tells me too. We have hardly spoken to each other. He has not apologized to me.

I now have to go into town for him to do some photocopying that he needs. I also had to go to the bank to withdraw some money for him to give to his gambling mate. He had driven me to town as my feet were very sore. When I came out of the bank, he was nowhere to be seen. I telephoned him and he had gone home. He couldn't be bothered to wait for me. My feet were killing me and I had to walk home. When I got indoors, I was very upset and told him that he didn't care about me and he was the selfish one as I had been helping him out. He started laughing and said it wasn't his fault. He is getting more annoyed now, saying that I don't care about his mother and I don't understand how ill she is. I told him she is physically in good shape and it is only her memory that is affected. I have caught him listening outside his mother's room in case I am being horrible to her.

I am getting terrible thoughts, wondering if there is any way I can get rid of him. Maybe I could put rat poison in his dinner. That wouldn't work though. An autopsy would show the contents of his stomach and show the poison. There are other things I could do but there is no point. I definitely do not want to go to prison. I'm sure he will get his comeuppance one day.

The last few years have gone so quickly and I feel I am a prisoner in my own home, looking after his mother twenty-four hours seven days a week. I'm unable to have a few days away to see my sister and she is not allowed to come to the house. I tell my sister that when his mother passes away, I will be free to come and go as I please. She says nothing will change and he will find another way to keep me tied down.

Nine years on and his mother has now passed away. He and his siblings have inherited the money from her property. He didn't offer me even a small amount for looking after her for all those years. What a selfish and money grabbing bastard he is. When my father passed away some years ago, he had purchased a self-made will and got my father to make me the sole benefactor for looking after him for about six months. My father didn't have much money but it should have been divided equally between my brothers, sisters and me. My brother had looked after him for about six years and my sister for three years after my mother had died.

All he thinks about is money and his gambling and he has said in the past that he doesn't give a shit about what people think. Selfish bastard.

I wish I could be strong like my sister and I know I should have listened to her many years ago. Looking back on my life, I think of all the opportunities that I have missed. I know deep down that I am frightened of him. I know if I left him, he would find me and possibly kill me. I would have no peace whatsoever. I know I am a fool to put up with all the crap I get from him most days.

Thinking back, I remember that when I first met him there was a physical attraction between us. I had been dating him for about a month when he told me he had a son with another woman. He said the woman had two other children and he only went with her for the sex. He did not want to be tied down with a ready-made family. I should have stayed working abroad and not come back to be with him. Maybe I was feeling a bit lost and didn't know anything about being a nanny to the Italian family.

He had asked me on several occasions to marry him and I said yes because he kept on and on. I remember I saved up to buy my own engagement ring because even then he was betting heavily on the horses. I think now how stupid I was then and how stupid I am now to put up with this marriage. I suppose I have stayed because of our children, for his family. I know my immediate family would have been proud of me if I had left. My brothers and sister have told me that they would always support me and I would always have a roof over my head.

To this day I am still in an abusive marriage, although he has mellowed a bit. I am always on my guard and just now let him rant and rave.

There is so much in the media about women being abused and sometimes murdered by their partners. He knows now that if he lays a hand on me, I will report him. My sister tells me that the way he speaks to me and the vile language he uses to me is classed as abuse and he should be reported to the police. My sister is convinced I don't tell her when he is abusive to me and she says that if she ever found out, there would be trouble and he would be toast!

She has now told me the best way to get evidence against him is to record his outburst and his tantrums on my mobile phone camera and send it to her.

I am now doing this which she will use as evidence should anything happen to me.

It is now coming up to my seventieth birthday. He has been away for two weeks and came back the day before my birthday. I was expecting maybe a small present which he could have bought in the duty-free shop on his way through the airport, but all I got was a card. I asked him if he had bought me a present and he said no and he wasn't going to.

He came back with Covid and was very poorly in bed. Maybe if he gets worse, they will cart him off to hospital. No such luck!

He continues to wish my family and in particular my sister nothing but bad luck and ill health. Hopefully he will be the one to suffer, not them.

Some years have now passed, why did I think that he may mellow in his old age, how many times have I been told by colleagues and family members, a Leopard never changes its spots?

As he ages he hasn't changed one bit, yet his coercive, controlling behaviour continues.

The physical abuse towards me has stopped, I think he knows better now as I did say to him, if you dare touch me again you will feel the full force of the law.

Of course he wouldn't want that, having a criminal record, he wouldn't want to end up in Prison again. That could work in my favour.

In the past when he used to hit me on several occasions, I used to feel numb afterwards and used to ask myself what did I do to deserve his anger towards me.

Trying to put my point across, he would not listen and he told me that I was stupid and that it was my own fault why he deserved to hit me as I made him angry.

Each time it happened I lost all love and respect I had for him.

I sometimes wonder how my life would have turned out if we had separated.

I am one hundred percent sure that he feels the same way.

My duty now is to cook, clean,and to wash his clothes for him.

There is very little affection towards him, even when going to bed at night , I might give him a quick kiss on his cheek, but no feelings back from him. I sometimes wonder why I bother.

Since the beginning of the New Year there has been times when he has kicked off, moaning about the towels on the radiator were not put on the way that he likes them, so a row starts and he shouts back at me telling me to leave and go and live with our son.

Anything mentioned, his family, then he calls me an argumentative cunt. Well that is nice language coming from him, what does he care about? This is the only language he knows.

During the cold winter weather he refuses to keep the radiators on for a long time, so turns them off and then opens the windows to let the cold air in. I am sure he is trying to make me ill by catching the flu, pneumonia or any other respiratory illness.

He tells me to keep the bedroom door closed at all times to keep the heat in, what's the point when the radiators are off anyway.

Where's his logic, he is stupid.

As there is no heat now in the bedroom, so he decides to get up in the night and put on the Halogen heater on all three bars as he now feels cold, of course these Halogen heaters are very bright and the brightness wakes me up, he is now asleep, so I get up and turn the heater down to one bar.

Of course all hell let loose in the morning when he wakes up, and shouts and screams at me for touching the heater, and that I was very selfish by not thinking of him.

As we live in a flat and we do not have the use of a garden, I have to dry the clothes on a clothes horse which is placed in the hallway.

He hates the washing hanging around, but I don't have any other option, my washing machine has a built in dryer he don't want me to use as it costs a lot, well what are my options I ask him.

He has now decided to order a Dry Buddy Heating system instead of using the dryer, well its up to him, I was quite happy using the clothes horse and drying them by the radiator.

We received the new heating system, and then the following week another one was delivered, now I have two.

He now tells me that it is my fault that he has ordered two, and would not admit up to his mistake.

Mysteriously the second one has now disappeared, what he has done with it god only knows.

He has now gone out and purchased a new exercise machine which cost a lot of money.

Christmas gone he tells me that he had no money and didn't offer a penny towards any of the extra Christmas food or gifts for the family members, he only handed me a small amount for our six grandchildren, which I believe he had won with his on-line gambling.

The screaming and shouting continues, he has not stopped going on about the way the towels are hung on the bathroom towel rail, we'll I've had enough so I now tell him that i will leave his towels on the bed and tell him to put them on the bathroom rail himself however he wants to hang them.

He has now told me that the extra dry buddy heating system that he ordered by mistake but wouldn't admit it, he is now giving this to our daughter.

He now calls me selfish and tells me that I don't care about him.

Well he has that right, how can you care and have respect for someone you have been married to for fifty years when you have had a marriage of hell.

I know that I could up and leave but then again all the bank cards, bank accounts, bank loans, are in my name, so he tells me that I am liable for these if anything happens to him.

Maybe I am frightened of what might be, but then on the other hand if this should happen I would have to declare myself bankrupt, as I don't have a penny to my name, or as they say " a pot to pee in"

He knows he has me over a barrel, although I do have the support from my sister and brothers but I don't want to put on them.

I suppose I am set in my ways and feel that if I should happen to walk away it would be too much of an upheaval where can I go, I don't want my sons to know what is going on although I do think that they all have a pretty good idea but not to the extent as it is and i believe this is why they don't say anything.

As for my daughter she is very much like her father so that would be a no no.

He spends most day watching television from early morning to late evening, all the old cowboy films, I never get a look in to any programmes that I want to watch. Selfish pig.

The only day I get a look in is if he goes to London for the day, peace and quite if not for long.

My sister tells me that I need to stay strong, why let him get away with it now at this time in my life, she says it's never too late to stand up for yourself.

Answer him back don't stand for his crap.

Easier said than done I tell her.

Deep down without admitting it to my sister I am frightened of what he might do, then he knows this, I expect that this is his whole idea to keep me on my toes making me feel that I am not worthy of having a peaceful life.

Perhaps it's the loyalty that I feel towards my marriage, my children and his family.

If I had enough strength and courage and I was in a good financial position, then I do believe that my life would change for the better. Maybe one day I may be in that position to up and leave.

He juggles money around from one account to the other.

Up until recently I always had cash to buy the weekly shopping, and kept a small amount back ,so that I could have an evening out at the local bingo evening with friends with the hope that I might have a small win.

Now he tells me that I have to buy the shopping with the credit card, I can't take any extra out for myself, he would question why I wanted an extra ten pounds in my purse.

As the abuse continues most days of the week, I decided to just ignore him when he starts ranting and raving about such trivial things.

By ignoring him and walking out of the room, he gets more wound up, as his ultimate aim is to start an argument, so that he thinks he is getting the upper hand, how pathetic he is, he is getting older and miserable.

I decided to run myself a bath. I am getting undressed in the bathroom and he now wants to put some antiseptic cream on his elbow, he shouts and tells me how to get into the bath, telling me that he is not interested in looking at me, so I now leave the bathroom and decided to wait to have my bath until he has finished.

He comes out and screams at me telling me that he is fed up and that he now knows what I think of him, and that we cannot continue the way we are, telling me that I now have to sleep in the spare room as I did not want to sleep next to him, so I tell him to sleep in the spare room. I have no intention of leaving my bed. He didn't speak for the rest of the day, that evening as I am getting ready for bed he asks me "why don't I sit with with him whilst he is watching television" I tell him why should I when he watches only what he wants to watch. I call him a selfish pig, he tells me to leave and go and live with my sister.

I wish I had the guts to get up and go and leave him on his own, I know that he needs me more that I need him, yes although he treats me as a skivvy

Now in my seventies, I will carry on as I am, I now go out to my bingo afternoon and sometimes on an evening, I have now have joined a ladies darts team at the local British Legion club, and one afternoon I go to short mat bowls and to table tennis club where I meet up with some of the local ladies who have become friends. I know he doesn't like me going out, he doesn't do anything other than sit on his arse all day long, he has no interests at all except watching the racing.

He makes out when he meets up with his cronies that all is good between us and makes out that he is a kind and considerate person, but if only they could see his true colours, and see what goes on behind closed doors.

My sister said that I should have a camera fitted somewhere in our front room to record all his screaming and shouting.

I have the last laugh on him in one aspect of my life, a few years past my sister inherited a small sum of money and shared it with me, placing some on investment for me but in her name, also giving me periodically a sum of money so now i don't have to struggle in the event if I need to buy myself anything . If he found out he would take it all from me to spend on his gambling so what I say "what he doesn't know won't hurt "well this is not his money or my money so if in the event he found out there is nothing he can do about it.

My sister has put in place a plan for the money she has in the event of my death. She will make sure that the money is split between my grandchildren.

I trust her completely, she is so kind and caring and I sometimes wish that I had taken her advice years ago.

My sister is so kind to me but concerned for me that I should have to live the rest of my life in the situation I am living in.

Looking back over my life throughout the years where I have suffered both physical and emotional abuse making me feel worthless, low self esteem and manipulated, humiliated, constant criticism by him, but there is one good thing he could not make me do, which he did ask me to do over the years, to lose all contact with my sister, this I refused to do and to this date he hates my sister with a vengeance, he hates the fact that she is in contact with our sons, and we are in contact at least 3 times a week, but he loves the fact that she don't speak to our daughter, my sister has no time for our daughter and on several occasions my sister knew how my daughter spoke to me, she is very much like her father. Arrogant, rude and a bad attitude. Sometimes I am ashamed to say that she is like this. He has no feelings towards me.

I was diagnosed with a growth on my forehead as being cancerous.

After many consultations and a biopsy with the doctors at my local hospital, I had to have the growth removed. This turned out to be cancerous.

I spent most of the day in daycare surgery.

He came and collected me late evening and as soon as we got inside he said there was nothing wrong with me so cook my dinner.

I was in a lot of pain as the injections I had were wearing off, I had to take extra strong painkillers to control the pain.

What a heartless pig he is, no sympathy whatsoever. If the shoe was on the other foot, he would want all the attention and as much sympathy you could give him.

Once my sister found out, she was fuming and called him all the names under the sun, she said that this should have been the final straw and that i should have refused to cook him a meal. Why didn't he go and get a takeaway and why should i have to put up with this. But what could I do.?.

I have been married to this man for over Fifty years now, and feel lucky that I am not recorded as a statistic of physical and emotional abuse, and as my life continues.I look back on our relationship maybe I should have reported him, the damage has been done and there will be no turning back,I have a lot of resentment and hostility towards him, he blames me as for everything that happens, yes as I am reminded by him I am a selfish wife and only think of myself.

He can continue to rant and rave for the rest of his life.

I do not care anymore.

Lovely words from my sister.

If only we could see ahead,

given a choice, maybe once or maybe twice.

Would your life be different in any way,

for the future we cannot see

dont wish for things

dont wish for what life may bring.

your life seems so unfair,

we cannot even share

the memories from when we were young

now a long time gone.

He has taken your life,

your happiness, no longer a wife,

but a slave trapped in

A Marriage from Hell.

www.ingramcontent.com/pod-product-compliance
Lightning Source LLC
Chambersburg PA
CBHW020325130626
46549CB00003B/1016